Improve your practice!

Piano Pre-Grade

Paul Harris

www.fabermusic.com/improve

© 2007 by Faber Music Ltd
This edition first published in 2007
3 Queen Square London WC1N 3AU
Music processing by Jackie Leigh
Design by Susan Clarke
Printed in England by Caligraving Ltd

ISBN10: 0-571-52844-9
EAN13: 978-0-571-52844-8

FABER _ff_ MUSIC

The secret of good practice!

Here's what to do to make your practice really fun and creative:

Before you start – cut out the playing cards

Find a pair of scissors and cut out the playing cards to size. They contain lots of interesting activities you can do with your pieces.

Be a musical detective

This book contains some lively new pieces for you to start your detective work on, using the *Explore Your Piece* pages provided. Further on are more blank *Explore Your Piece* pages which you can photocopy and use to investigate pieces in your other books.

Whenever you start a new piece (from this book, or one of your own) begin by searching the music for clues to help you practise and play it really well. Answer the questions in the *Explore Your Piece* sections. You may like to do this in one go, or you can spread your detective work over a few days.

This is how each practice session should go:

Warm-ups

Begin each practice with some warm-ups. There are already a few examples for you to choose from and your teacher can add some more.

Activities without the music

Deal yourself one or two cards from the **Without Music** pack and work through the activities *without looking at the music!*

Activities with the music

Now deal yourself one or two cards from the **With Music** pack and work through the activities with the music open.

You choose

Complete your practice with some more activities of your own choice. Playing other pieces, working at some scales, working at improving your sight reading or perhaps composing a piece. Keep thinking about what the week's special ingredient might be (see page 23).

important

You may want to concentrate on just one piece in a practice session, or perhaps work at several. Deal yourself different cards for each piece.

Warm-ups

Before you begin practising, you need to warm-up – both your fingers and your brain! Here are a few examples to get you started. Ask your teacher to add more for you to choose from.

1	Check your posture. Are you sitting correctly?
2	Have a glass of water. Water is just about the best brain food there is! Begin your practice with a small glass (or half a glass) of water and you'll be working at your best!
3	Play very evenly and repeat at least 3 times.
4	Play very evenly and repeat at least 3 times.
5	Play very evenly and repeat at least 3 times.
6	Play very evenly and repeat at least 3 times.
7	
8	
9	
10	

Explore your piece

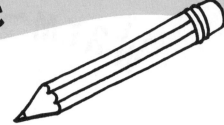

Here's the first piece for you to try out your new kind of practice! Have a look at it (but don't begin to play it yet), then go on to some detective work. Read the questions and then fill in the boxes.

Have a cup of tea!

Paul Harris

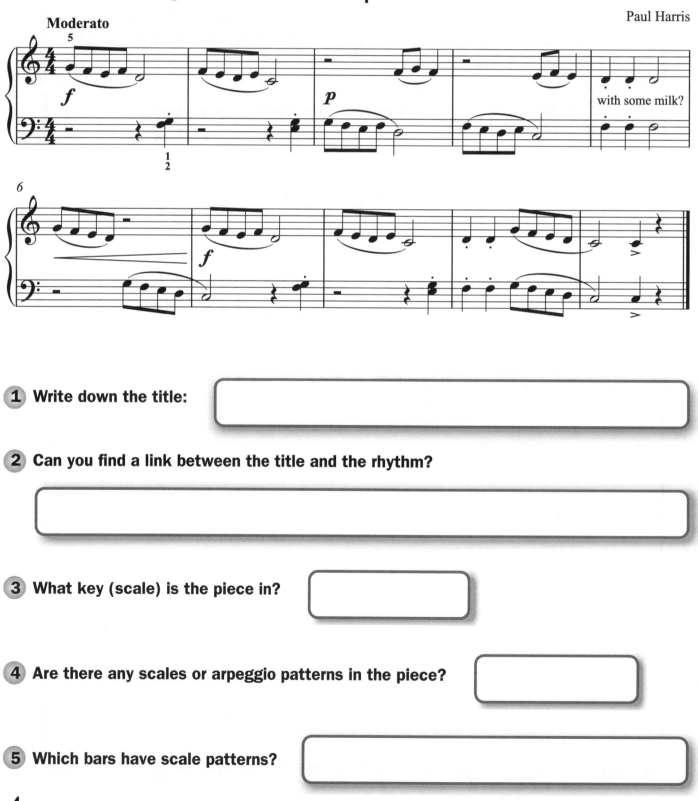

with some milk?

1. **Write down the title:**

2. **Can you find a link between the title and the rhythm?**

3. **What key (scale) is the piece in?**

4. **Are there any scales or arpeggio patterns in the piece?**

5. **Which bars have scale patterns?**

4

All your answers form the 'ingredients' of your piece. If you don't understand a question, don't worry: just remember to ask your teacher in your next lesson.

6 Does the opening melody go mostly up or down?

7 What is the time signature?

8 What will you count?

9 Write down the dynamic markings.

10 Write down any other markings (such as the Italian word at the beginning, slurs, *crescendos*, accents, *staccatos*) and what they mean.

11 Think of some words that could describe the mood or character of the piece (you might like to answer this question after you've been learning the piece for a while or after your teacher has played the piece to you).

If you've filled in all the boxes, well done: good detective work! Now deal yourself one or two cards from each pile, first from the Without Music set, then from the With Music set. Follow the instructions and off you go with some really fun and creative practice on Have a cup of tea!

Explore your piece

Here's another piece. Have a look at it (but don't begin to play it yet), then go on to a bit of detective work! Look at the questions and then fill in the boxes.

The cool wizard!

Pam Wedgwood

1. Write down the title:

2. Write down the composer's name:

3. Can you find out something about the composer? Ask your teacher or try your library or the internet.

4. What is the time signature?

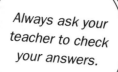

Always ask your teacher to check your answers.

5 What will you count?

6 Write down all the dynamic markings (including *dim.* and *cresc.* markings).

7 Write down any other markings (such as slurs, accents and *staccatos*) and what they mean.

8 Write down some words that you think best describe the mood or character of the piece.

9 Are there any repeated rhythms in the piece? Write them down here:

10 Are there any bars in the piece which will need special practice?

Now deal yourself one or two cards from each pile, first from the Without Music set, then from the With Music set. Follow the instructions and off you go with some really fun and creative practice on **The cool wizard***!*

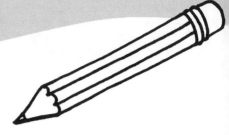

Explore your piece

Here's the next piece. Have a look at it (but don't begin to play it yet), then go on to a bit of detective work! Look at the questions and then fill in the boxes.

A waltz that halts

Paul Harris

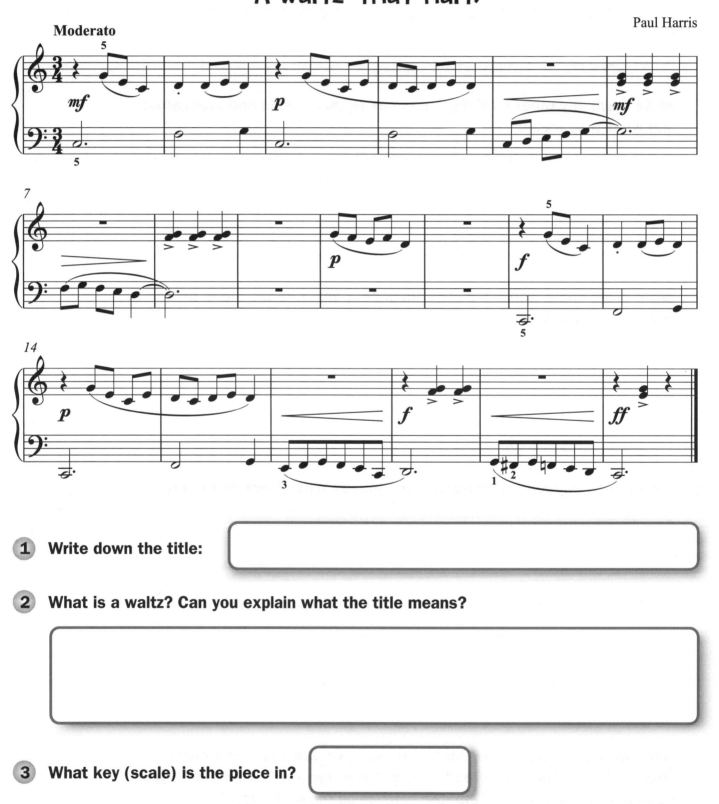

1 Write down the title:

2 What is a waltz? Can you explain what the title means?

3 What key (scale) is the piece in?

4 Which bars have scale patterns?

5 Which bars have arpeggio patterns?

6 What is the time signature?

7 What will you count?

8 Write down all the dynamic markings.

9 Write down any other markings (such the Italian word at the beginning, slurs, accents and *staccatos*) and what they mean.

10 Think of some words that could describe the mood or character of the piece (you might like to answer this question after you've been learning the piece for a while or after your teacher has played the piece to you).

Now deal yourself one or two cards from each pile, first from the Without Music set, then from the With Music set. Follow the instructions and off you go with some really fun and creative practice on A waltz that halts!

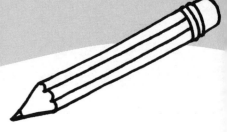

Here's your next piece. Get searching for those ingredients and fill in the boxes!

Buses always come in threes

Paul Harris

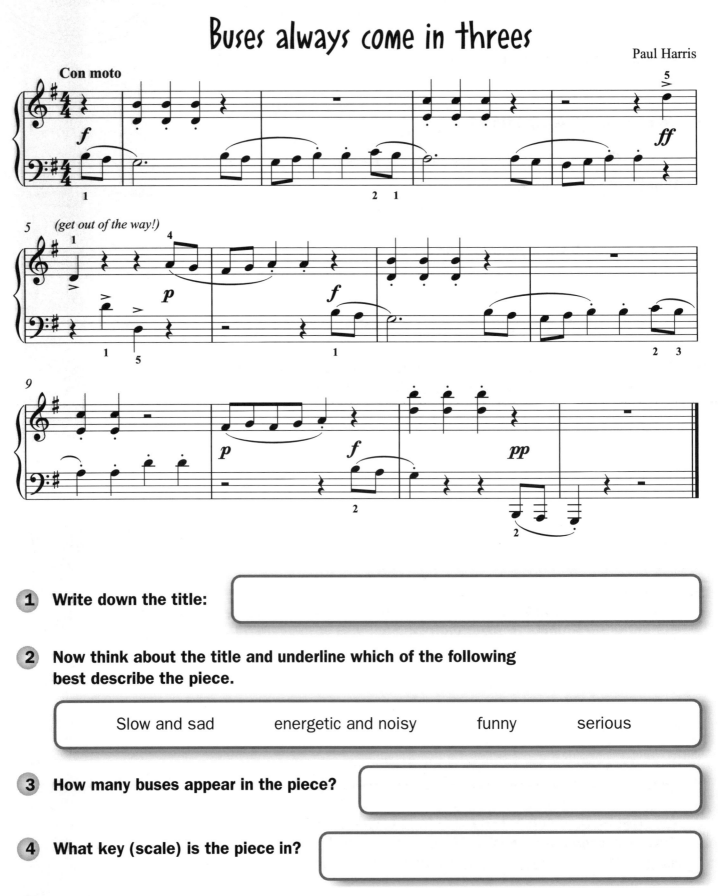

1. **Write down the title:**

2. **Now think about the title and underline which of the following best describe the piece.**

   Slow and sad   energetic and noisy   funny   serious

3. **How many buses appear in the piece?**

4. **What key (scale) is the piece in?**

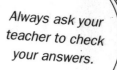
5   **What is the time signature?**

6   **What will you count?**

7   **Write down all the dynamic markings. List them in order from soft to loud.**

8   **Write down any other markings (such as the Italian word at the beginning, slurs, accents and *staccatos*) and what they mean.**

9   **Do you think any of the bars might be tricky and need some special practice? Which bars?**

Now deal yourself one or two cards from each pile, first from the Without Music set, then from the With Music set. Follow the instructions and off you go with some really fun and creative practice on Buses always come in threes!

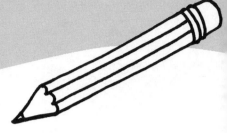

Explore your piece

Here's your next piece. Ready for some detective work?

Country dance

Daniel Gottlob Türk

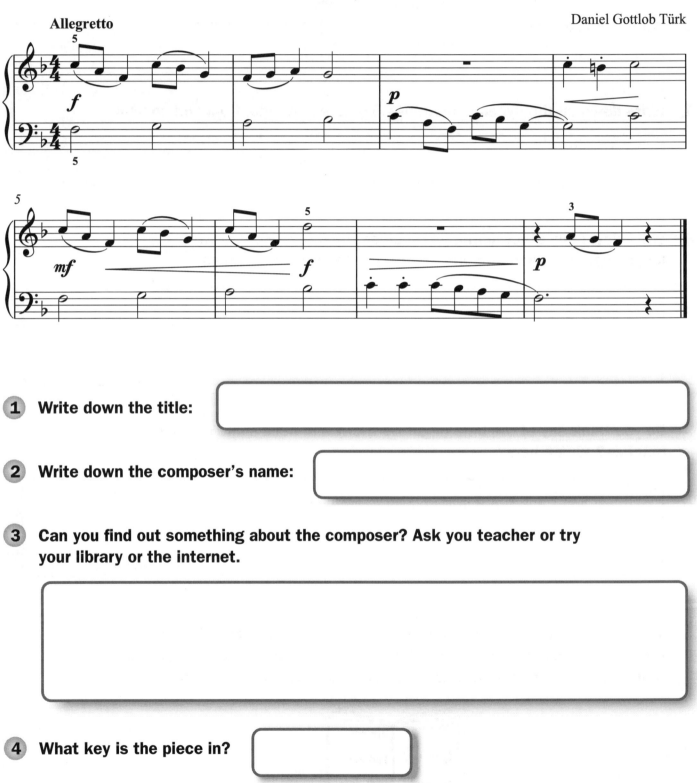

1 Write down the title:

2 Write down the composer's name:

3 Can you find out something about the composer? Ask you teacher or try your library or the internet.

4 What key is the piece in?

5 Write the key signature here (try writing the clef too!):

6 In which bars are there scale or arpeggio patterns?

7 What is the time signature?

8 What will you count?

9 Write down all the dynamic markings (including *dim.* and *cresc.* markings).

10 Write down any other markings (such as the Italian word at the beginning, slurs, *staccatos*, ties and accidentals) and what they mean.

11 Write down some words that you think best describe the mood or character of the piece.

12 Are there any tricky rhythms that need extra practice in the piece? Write them down here:

Now deal yourself one or two cards from each pile, first from the Without Music set, then from the With Music set. Follow the instructions and off you go with some really fun and creative practice on Country dance!

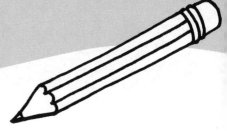

Explore your piece

Here's your next piece. Get searching for those ingredients!

It's cosy and warm by the fire

Paul Harris

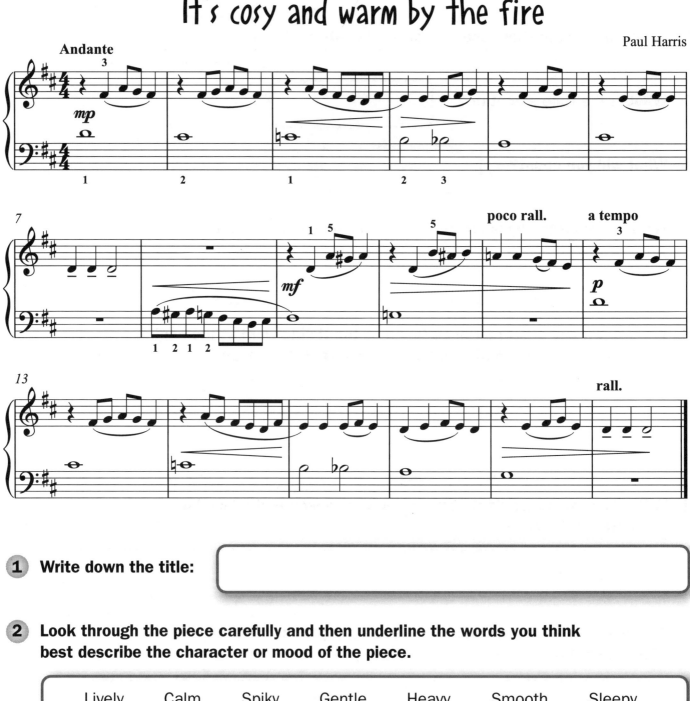

1 Write down the title:

2 Look through the piece carefully and then underline the words you think best describe the character or mood of the piece.

Lively   Calm   Spiky   Gentle   Heavy   Smooth   Sleepy

3 What key (scale) is the piece in?

4 Which notes are affected by the key signature?

14

5 In which bars can you find scale patterns?

6 What is the time signature?

7 What will you count?

8 Write down all the dynamic markings. List them in order from soft to loud.

9 Write down all other markings (such as Italian words, slurs and musical symbols) and what they mean.

10 Do you think any of the bars might need some special practice? Which bars?

Now deal yourself one or two cards from each pile, first from the Without Music set, then from the With Music set. Follow the instructions and off you go with some really fun and creative practice on It's cosy and warm by the fire*!*

Explore your piece

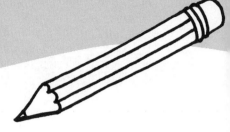

Here's your next piece. Get ready for some more detective work …

Owls, wizards and broomsticks

Paul Harris

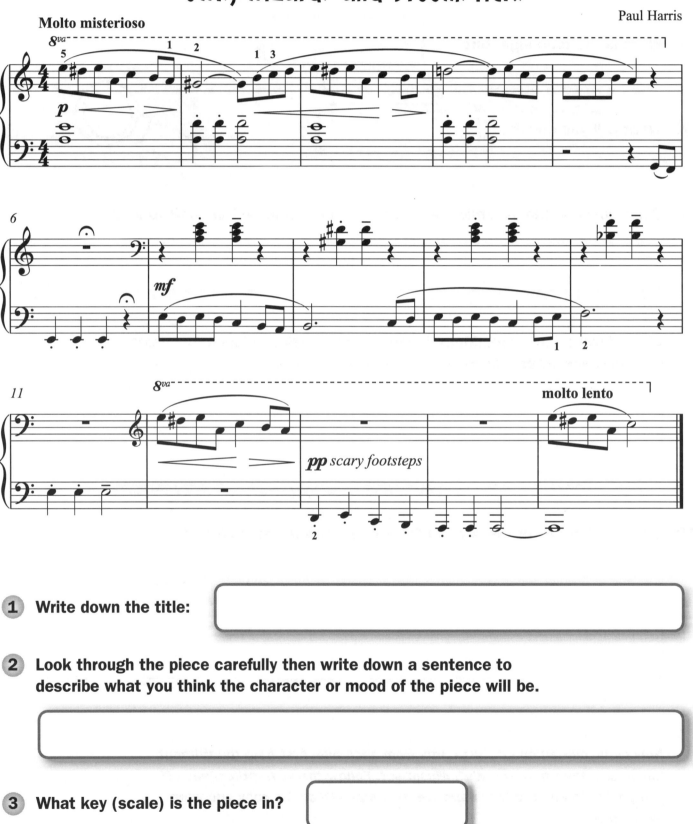

1 **Write down the title:**

2 **Look through the piece carefully then write down a sentence to describe what you think the character or mood of the piece will be.**

3 **What key (scale) is the piece in?**

4 Which bars use scale patterns?

5 What is the time signature?

6 What will you count?

7 Write down all the dynamic markings. List them in order from soft to loud.

8 Write down any other markings (such as the Italian words, slurs and *staccatos*) and what they mean.

9 Do you think any of the bars might need some special practice? Which bars?

10 Can you spot some interesting ingredients in this piece? (Here are some clues: clef changes and chords.) Write them below, with the bars they are in.

Now deal yourself one or two cards from each pile, first from the Without Music set, then from the With Music set. Follow the instructions and off you go with some really fun and creative practice on Owls, wizards and broomsticks!

Explore your piece

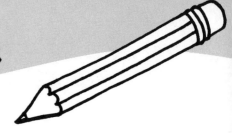

Now you can choose your own pieces to practise. Do your careful detective work first and find all the ingredients.

1 Write down the title:

2 Write down the composer's name:

3 Can you find out something about the composer (dates, place of birth, titles of other pieces)? Ask your teacher or try the internet or your library.

4 What key is the piece in?

5 Write the key signature here (try writing the clef too):

6 Are there any scale and arpeggio patterns in the piece?

7 In which bars do they occur?

8 What is the time signature?

9 What will you count?

10 Write down all the dynamic markings (including *dim.* and *cresc.* markings).
List them in order from soft to loud.

11 Write down any other markings (such as Italian words, slurs, accents
and *staccatos*) and what they mean.

12 Write down some words that you think best describe the mood or
character of the piece:

13 Are there any tricky rhythms in the piece? Write them down here:

14 Are there any tricky finger patterns in the piece?
Which bars will need special practice?

*Now deal yourself one or two cards from each pile, first from the Without
Music set, then from the With Music set. Follow the instructions and off
you go with some really fun and creative practice!*

Explore your piece

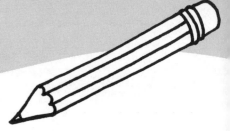

Now you can choose your own pieces to practise. Do your careful detective work first and find all the ingredients.

1 Write down the title:

2 Write down the composer's name:

3 Can you find out something about the composer (dates, place of birth, titles of other pieces)? Ask your teacher or try the internet or your library.

4 What key is the piece in?

5 Write the key signature here (try writing the clef too):

6 Are there any scale and arpeggio patterns in the piece?

7 In which bars do they occur?

8 What is the time signature?

9 What will you count?

10 Write down all the dynamic markings (including *dim.* and *cresc.* markings).
List them in order from soft to loud.

11 Write down any other markings (such as Italian words, slurs, accents
and *staccatos*) and what they mean.

12 Write down some words that you think best describe the mood or
character of the piece:

13 Are there any tricky rhythms in the piece? Write them down here:

14 Are there any tricky finger patterns in the piece?
Which bars will need special practice?

*Now deal yourself one or two cards from each pile, first from the Without
Music set, then from the With Music set. Follow the instructions and off
you go with some really fun and creative practice!*

Ingredients library

You can build up a useful list of 'ingredients' here by writing down all the terms and symbols which you discover in your pieces, followed by what they mean.

Practice diary

As your practice develops each week choose what you would like to be your **special ingredient**. It may, for example, be one of the following:
- Part or all of one of your pieces that you can play really well.
- An improvisation (one that you can remember!).
- A scale (or part of a scale) that you can play really well.
- Your own composition.
- A tricky passage you've mastered.

Lesson Write the lesson number or date here:	Teacher's bit Your teacher may want to jot down some ideas for your practice this week.	Parent's bit Your parents may like to write a comment or message for your teacher.	Your bit For you to write down your *special ingredient*.

Parents' page

How long should a practice session last?

Try to avoid setting a particular time-frame for practice. This tends to encourage clock-watching and time-filling! Instead encourage your child to decide what they would like to achieve in each practice and then take as much time as they need to do it. This is a much more thoughtful approach that will result in more focussed work.

'I'm too tired to practise today.'

There are lots of alternative activities you can suggest:
- Practise away from the piano: sit down with the piece and 'hear it' silently (it's not difficult). Think particularly about the character of the music.
- Listen to some music – anything is acceptable, but the catch is that a sentence or two must be written afterwards about the music. Whether it was fast or slow, loud or soft, lively or calm, cheerful or miserable, high or low, what instruments were playing, and so on. This is very good aural training!
- Do a **PEP** analysis on the piece being learnt:
  P is for problems: decide what problems still have to be solved at the next practice. Make a note of them.
  E is for expression – what character is the piece trying to convey?
  P is for practice – the next practice! Write down what particular work will be done.
  It's surprising but a PEP analysis often leads to some real practice!
- Clean the piano (with a duster, not a bucket and water)!
- Do just one minute's practice (a cunning ploy as this often leads to more).
- Some free improvisation – anything you like!

How should I reward practice?

The best rewards of good practice should be much warm praise and your child's growing awareness that they are making really good progress and pleasing both you and their teacher. An *occasional* 'prize' (try to make it something musical like an appropriate CD, some new music, or an outing to a concert) is okay!